Wha[t] [Is] the Women's World Cup?

by Gina Shaw

illustrated by Ted Hammond

Penguin Workshop

This one's for Jaxon,
the newest member of our family!—GS

To my kids, Stephanie and Jason—TH

PENGUIN WORKSHOP
An imprint of Penguin Random House LLC, New York

First published in the United States of America by Penguin Workshop,
an imprint of Penguin Random House LLC, New York, 2023

Visit us online at penguinrandomhouse.com.

Library of Congress Cataloging-in-Publication Data is available.

Printed in the United States of America

ISBN 9780593520659 (paperback)   10 9 8 7 6 5 4 3 2 1 WOR
ISBN 9780593520666 (library binding)   10 9 8 7 6 5 4 3 2 1 WOR

Contents

What Is the Women's World Cup?

On July 5, 2015, more than fifty thousand soccer fans were just settling into their seats at BC Place Stadium in Vancouver, Canada. They were there to watch the final game of the Women's World Cup. It was Japan vs. the United States.

These same teams had played in the final in 2011, and now they were playing again four years later.

In 2011, Japan had beaten the United States. Would they be able to repeat the victory?

If you didn't arrive on time to the game, this is what you would have missed. In the third minute,

Carli Lloyd, the captain of Team USA, rushed down the pitch (the playing field) and directed a well-placed corner kick from Megan Rapinoe into the net. A corner kick is a free kick from the corner of the pitch. This goal was the fastest one ever made in a Women's World Cup final. The score, United States 1–Japan 0.

Next, US team member Lauren Holiday took a penalty kick. (This happens when the other team has broken a rule.) At first, Japan's defenders kept the ball from going in. But they bungled it in front of the goal. Lloyd slipped into the confusion and gently tapped the ball into the net. Only five minutes into the game Carli Lloyd had scored the second goal! The score was now United States 2–Japan 0. A goal by Holiday fourteen minutes in made it 3–0.

And just when the spectators thought they could take a moment to catch their breath, Carli Lloyd did it again! At midfield, she pounded her foot against the ball as hard as she could. That sent it soaring halfway across the length of the pitch. The crowd went wild! It was an astonishing goal. It gave Carli Lloyd the first hat trick (three goals made by the same player in a single game) in the final of a Women's World Cup. The score: United States 4–Japan 0.

Team USA scored one more goal. Despite Japan getting two goals, the final score was 5–2. Team USA won! Lloyd was named Player of the Match.

It was an unforgettable Women's World Cup!

The Pitch

The pitch is the rectangular playing field for soccer games. It can be made of grass or artificial turf. However, the color must be green.

A goal is centered at both ends of the field. The pitch is divided into two halves by the halfway line. In the middle of this halfway line is the center spot. Around it is a circle. Opposing players are not allowed to enter the center circle when the other team kicks off.

Within the pitch, there are markings for the penalty area, the center spot for kickoffs, and the corners for corner kicks. The ball is in play as long as it is inside the end lines and sidelines. The ball must cross the goal line to be a goal. If the ball passes over the sidelines, it is out-of-bounds.

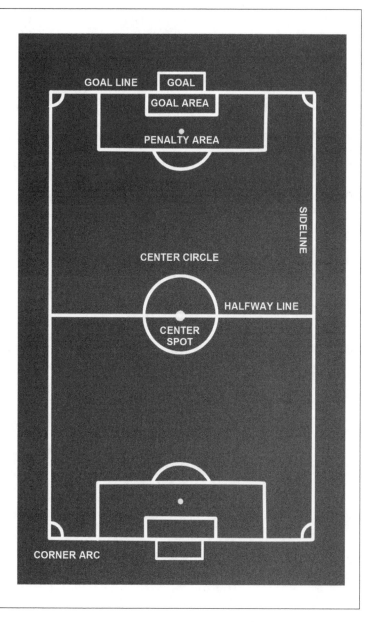

In 1999, the Women's World Cup was played in the United States for the first time. Since then, women's soccer has become incredibly popular in this country among kids and teens. There are more than three million soccer players in the United States between the ages of five and nineteen, and about 1.4 million of them are female.

CHAPTER 1
First, a Bit of History

Soccer, or football as it is called in many countries including England, is the most popular sport around the world. It has a very long history. It can be traced back more than two thousand years to Asia, the Americas, and Europe. But the modern-day version of the game began in England.

There, in 1863, the Football Association (FA) was formed. It set rules for the game. These include forbidding tripping opponents or touching the ball with the hands. At first, football was entertainment for the British working class. By the late nineteenth century as many as thirty thousand people would come to watch the big matches. As the popularity of the sport grew,

women wanted to play. They wanted to create women's teams and leagues. Would they be allowed to do this?

The Football Association would not get involved. They had set the rules for men's games only.

In the late 1800s, women didn't have the same rights as men. They were expected to be proper and ladylike and stay at home to care for their families. They were not supposed to be running around a muddy football field.

But women were determined to take part in the sport they enjoyed.

The first women's international match took place in 1881 when England played against Scotland. Between 1881 and 1897, more than 120 organized matches were recorded. But there still wasn't an organization, like the FA, to watch over and record matches or tournaments. Then, in 1895, a woman who called herself Nettie Honeyball (her real name may have been Mary Hutson) started the British Ladies' Football Club. Honeyball placed ads in newspapers to encourage women to play football. She often said that "women are not ornamental and useless creatures" and that "the manly game could be a womanly game as well."

Nettie Honeyball

On March 23, 1895, the first women's match that played by FA rules took place in London. The women's teams represented North and South London. The match was advertised in newspapers. About twelve thousand people came to watch.

Many of the onlookers cheered, but lots of others shouted awful things at the players. Several newspapers ran articles making fun of the women players' appearance and the way they dressed.

None of this stopped Nettie Honeyball, though. She took the British Ladies' Football Club on a tour of England. The women played

on men's fields and in men's stadiums.

Unfortunately, by the end of the tour, only a few hundred fans were showing up. The first attempt to make women's football popular was not a success. What was going to happen to women's football?

No one was quite sure.

CHAPTER 2
A War Changes Everything

World War I began in 1914 after the murder of an Austro-Hungarian nobleman. This terrible war lasted from 1914 through most of 1918. Strangely, it helped to save women's football in Britain.

As British men went off to fight, women took over their jobs in factories across the country. Many made military supplies and equipment. The factories were filled with dangerous machinery and harmful chemicals. Some factory owners thought it might be good for the women workers to play football during their lunch and dinner breaks. It would keep them strong and healthy.

Were the factory owners doing this to support women's football?

The Two Sides of World War I

Most World War I battles took place in Europe, Africa, and the Middle East. Germany, Austria-Hungary, Bulgaria, and the Ottoman Empire banded together on one side. They called themselves the Central Powers. These countries fought against Britain, France, Serbia, Russia, Italy, Romania, Japan, and eventually, the United States. They were known as the Allied Powers. By September 1918 the Allied Powers had won the war.

Not exactly. They thought it would help the women do their jobs better!

Soon these women began to set up football teams. Their games raised money for charity and the war effort. One team became extremely popular and successful. The team was named for the factory where the players worked—a train manufacturer called Dick, Kerr and Co.

The workers of Dick, Kerr and Co.

The team was started in 1917. It drew ten thousand people to its very first match, and, over time, helped to make women's football a real sport in its own right.

That year, on the day after Christmas, the first England vs. Ireland game took place. There was an England vs. Scotland match the following year, and in 1920, England played France. Women's football was growing in popularity even outside of Britain. When the Dick, Kerr's Ladies played against the

St. Helens' Ladies on December 26, 1920, fifty-three thousand fans came to watch. More than fourteen thousand fans were turned away. This was the largest crowd ever for a women's football game in Britain. This record lasted for more than ninety years, until the London Olympics in 2012.

Lily Parr

Lily Parr of the Dick, Kerr's Ladies team was one of the greatest players of all time. She was the fourth of seven children and grew up playing football and rugby with her brothers. In 1919, she was recruited to the Dick, Kerr's Ladies. She was close to six feet tall and only fourteen years old at the time! A teammate said Parr had "a kick like a mule." Parr scored forty-three goals in her first season.

Between the years of 1917 to 1921, there were about 150 women's teams in England. The women had become genuine celebrities. But by the end of 1921, disaster struck for women's football.

What a Team! What a Team Player!

All in all, the Dick, Kerr's Ladies played 828 matches. They lost only 24 games. Lily Parr scored nearly a thousand goals for her team in her career! Parr played against both male and female teams. It is said that one time, she accidentally broke the wrist of a male goalie with the force of her ball.

Lily Parr died at the age of seventy-three in May 1978. In 2002, Parr was the first female to be inducted into the National Football Museum's Hall of Fame in Manchester, England. In 2019, a statue of her was placed there.

The women's teams got *too* popular. Men had steadily been returning home from war and taking back their jobs. Women were forced back into their homes to care for their families.

Not only did the men take back their jobs, they also didn't want women playing what they still considered their sport. The popularity of women's football had become a threat to men's football. The men's teams didn't draw nearly as many fans. The FA now changed their view of women's football again. Doctors were consulted. Dr. Mary Scharlieb, a London physician, said, "I consider it a most unsuitable game, too much for a woman's physical frame."

On December 5, 1921, the FA banned women from playing the game. The organization stopped them from using the men's pitches and facilities. FA referees were told they could no longer work at women's matches.

Soon the growth of the men's game surpassed the women's game. Other countries, including Norway in 1931, France in 1932, Brazil in 1941, and West Germany in 1955 joined the FA ban. From then on, women's football was played only

occasionally for charity events.

The ban resulted in a terrible setback for women's football.

Football in Brazil

South America

Soccer is hugely popular in Brazil. The first women's football matches played in Brazil were in 1913. Then, in 1921, two women's teams from São Paulo played in the first organized women's football game. By the early 1930s, more Brazilian women and girls joined the game. In 1940, the interest in women's football increased, and women were allowed to play in big stadiums in São Paulo until their ban came along in 1941.

CHAPTER 3
A Comeback!

It wasn't until 1971 that the FA lifted the ban on women's football in England. Other countries, including West Germany, Brazil, and France eventually lifted their bans, too. But for half a century, tremendous damage had been done to women's football.

In the 1970s, the fight for women's rights was gaining support around the world. Women

wanted the same opportunities for good jobs as men. They wanted to be paid as much money as men for doing the same jobs.

And what did women soccer players want? They wanted to play their game and be respected for the amazing athletes they were! Women's teams across Europe, Asia, and the Americas began to play more soccer games with other teams in other

countries. A women's world tournament took place in Italy in 1970. Then, in 1971, a second one took place in Mexico City. This women's tournament was an enormous success. At the final game, more than 110,000 spectators gathered in Azteca Stadium!

Did this mark a final turning point for women's football? Unfortunately, no.

Mexico City, 1971

A New US Law—Title IX

On June 23, 1972, the United States Congress passed a law called the Educational Amendments of 1972. One part of the law, known as Title IX, stated that schools and universities that received money from the federal government had to offer

girls the same opportunities to play sports as boys had. Before Title IX, girls' sports had often been ignored. Now young women were encouraged to play sports. Women's soccer exploded! It was (and still is) one of the most popular sports for girls to play.

Very slowly, change came about. The world organization, Fédération Internationale de Football Association (FIFA), got involved with women's football. Finally in 1974, FIFA approved a women's tournament. It was called the Nordic Championship and was played in Finland. Still, by the end of 1975, only thirty-six international games had been played. By 1979, 125 games were played.

These numbers, however, didn't tell the whole story. Many more matches were being played unofficially. They weren't recorded. A governing body was badly needed for women's football.

In 1986, for the first time in its history, a woman was invited to speak at the FIFA Congress. Ellen Wille was from Norway. She had fought for years to get women's football recognized in her home country. Now she wanted to continue her fight internationally. She called for the creation of a Women's Football World Cup.

What Does FIFA Do?

FIFA is soccer's governing group. It organizes major international tournaments. The most famous for men is the FIFA World Cup.

For women soccer players, the FIFA Women's World Cup is the most important competition. FIFA organizes the World Cup every four years. So far, the most successful team in the Women's World Cup has been the United States, with four titles.

FIFA World Cup   FIFA Women's World Cup

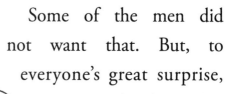

Ellen Wille

Some of the men did not want that. But, to everyone's great surprise, FIFA voted and agreed to Wille's demands. Ellen Wille became known as the Mother of Modern-Day Women's Football!

In 1988, in Guangdong, China, FIFA put the idea for a Women's World Cup to the test. Twelve teams from around the world competed. They were placed in groups called confederations. Each represented a different part of the world. It wasn't big news, though. Back then, there was hardly any publicity for the women's game.

FIFA watched this trial tournament closely. What would happen if it turned out to be a disaster?

There might never be a Women's World Cup. But what if the trial was a success?

FIFA would create a Women's World Cup!

The stakes could not have been higher. Fortunately, the tournament turned out to be a success. Attendance was strong, as was interest by soccer fans worldwide. FIFA was on its way to holding the first Women's World Cup!

Soccer Confederations

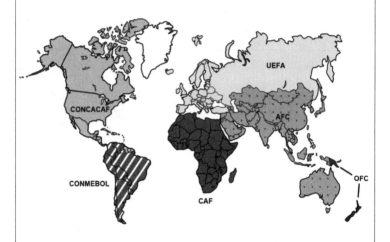

    In international soccer, the world is broken up into six regions called *confederations*. The teams within each confederation compete against one another in order to earn a World Cup spot. This process is called *qualifying*. The number of spots given to each confederation varies greatly.

CHAPTER 4
Let the Games Begin

As promised, in 1991, FIFA held the first Women's World Cup tournament from November 16 to November 30. It took place in Guangdong, China. (FIFA selected China as the host because the trial tournament in 1988 had been held there. Stadiums were already built.) The tournament was only broadcast on Chinese TV. If the tournament didn't work out well, the rest of the world wouldn't learn too much about it.

FIFA did not want to use the words *World Cup* in the tournament title. It named the event the "First FIFA World Championship for Women's Football for the M&M's Cup." Why?

FIFA was still hesitant that this competition might not be worthy of the "World Cup" name. Also, with this title, FIFA was able to honor its corporate sponsor, Mars, Inc., the maker of M&M's candy. (A sponsor is a company that helps pay for an event.)

For this first World Cup, FIFA changed some of the rules from the men's game. The reason they did this was they didn't think women could handle a ninety-minute match or a tournament that lasted over a month. On the plus side, though, six female referees and assistant referees were assigned to matches for the first time in FIFA history.

The USWNT (US Women's National Team) came into this tournament with their intense,

The first all-female referee team

forward-attacking line of Michelle Akers, Carin Jennings, and captain April Heinrichs. The Chinese press nicknamed these three players the "Triple-Edged Sword." The United States also had nineteen-year-old Mia Hamm.

In the group stage, the United States beat Sweden, 3–2, but that didn't mean Sweden was out of the tournament. (The way teams are eliminated in World Cup soccer tournaments is very complicated.) Next, the United States defeated Brazil, 5–0, with goals made by Heinrichs (2), Jennings (1), Akers (1), and Hamm (1).

Carin Jennings   April Heinrichs

In the quarterfinals game, Michelle Akers scored five goals for the United States! She would

Michelle Akers

later recall, "It was like wow, wow, wow, good, oh my gosh. It was sort of mind-blowing."

In the Team USA vs. Germany semifinal game, Carin Jennings scored a hat trick in the first thirty-three minutes of the first half. Her second goal was kicked from twenty-five yards away—the length of a regulation swimming pool in the United States! April Heinrichs scored two

more goals in the second half and the United
States beat Germany, 5–2.

Team USA moved on to the final game against
Norway. Twenty minutes in, Michelle Akers
scored a header (a ball that a player hits with her
head). It was made off a free kick by midfielder

United States vs. Germany, 1991

Shannon Higgins. Norway's Linda Medalen tied the game 1–1 at minute twenty-nine. Then, in the second half, Akers scored the game-winning goal, her tenth of the tournament, only two minutes before the end of the game! Akers won the Golden Boot. The Golden Boot is given for the most goals scored throughout the tournament.

In front of sixty thousand fans, and wearing uniforms sourced from a men's team's practice outfit, the US women defeated Norway to win the first FIFA World Championship for women. In fact, not only did the women's team win the championship, they never lost a game during the two-week tournament. They outscored their opponents by a combined score of 25–5. US Coach Anson Dorrance said, "I feel what we've done here is proof to the world we are a developing soccer nation." The US team couldn't wait to share their victory with their fans back home.

But there was a major problem. Hardly anyone in the United States knew that the tournament had taken place or that the United States had won. Michelle Akers said, only "four people met our plane at the gate when we landed at JFK." And one was a friend of hers!

Michelle Akers

Michelle Akers is one of the greatest women's soccer players of all time. She was named FIFA Female Player of the Century by FIFA officials in 2000. On the field, Akers was a powerhouse. She is the fourth all-time leading scorer in the World Cup.

Not only did Michelle Akers fight on the field, but she fought against inequality off the field as well. Before the 1999 Women's World Cup, the team had to train on concrete. No pitches were available to them. The playing conditions were terrible. Right before the 1996 Olympic Games, the US team went on strike. As Akers said, "It wasn't like we were even on strike for a million dollars. It was just like 'Can we have money for childcare? Can you pay our rent?'" A bitter battle took place. At that time, the team did settle some of their disputes with the US Soccer Federation and competed in the Olympics. They won the gold medal!

Unfortunately, Akers had injured herself many times throughout her career. She had twelve knee surgeries, had lost teeth, had suffered from concussions, and had developed chronic fatigue syndrome. Sadly, she never fully recovered and retired in 2000.

Michelle Akers helped change the game of soccer at a time when female athletes were considered second-class athletes.

When FIFA'S president saw just how successful the 1991 Women's World Cup was, he wrote, "women's football is now well and truly established." With ninety-nine goals scored throughout the tournament, the women's game proved it could be even more exciting than the men's game. And so the tournament was renamed the Women's World Cup, and FIFA continues to hold it every four years.

FIFA president João Havelange

However, all the US players received was a note of congratulations with a $500 bonus check. This was at a time when FIFA offered prize money of around $50 million to split among the men's World Cup team winners!

CHAPTER 5
The Photo Seen Round the World

On July 10, the final game of the 1999 Women's World Cup was played. The tournament, hosted by the United States, took place at the sold-out Rose Bowl in Pasadena, California. A record number of spectators—

90,185—were about to witness the two best teams and longtime rivals—the Chinese People's Republic and the United States of America—play against each other. At the 1996 Olympics, Team USA had defeated China 2–1 and won the gold medal. Now China wanted to even things up.

Singer Jennifer Lopez got the party started by performing her new song "Let's Get Loud" before the final began. Lopez's career was just taking off and this song became one of her most well-known. The stadium was really revved up by the time the teams kicked off.

The '99ers

There was extensive TV and media coverage, with more than forty million viewers tuning in. Nicknamed the '99ers, Team USA had an incredible lineup of players, several of whom had played in previous World Cups—Michelle Akers, Mia Hamm, Briana Scurry, Julie Foudy, Kristine Lilly, and Brandi Chastain, among others. Defender Carla Overbeck was the captain.

Joy Fawcett, Kate Markgraf, Brandi Chastain, and Overbeck formed a solid defense that only allowed three goals throughout the tournament.

China, however, had Sun Wen. Wen had

Sun Wen

scored China's only goal against the United States when the two teams played against each other in the Olympics.

Unbelievably, based on the strength of these two teams, there was no score at the end of ninety minutes. That meant the two teams had to play up to thirty minutes of extra time. The team that scored first would win. This is known as a Golden Goal. Imagine the kind of pressure this puts on players!

Fan Yunjie of China had the best chance of making a goal. But her header was blocked by Kristine Lilly. After the thirty minutes of extra time, the score still remained the same, 0–0. Now, the 1999 Women's World Cup was going to be decided by a penalty shoot-out. In a penalty shoot-out, each team has five chances to score. It's kicker against keeper. Being a goalkeeper is the hardest position in soccer. It is both mentally and physically challenging. Goalies must perform under extreme pressure.

Fan Yunjie

Briana Scurry

China won the coin toss and chose to shoot first. Xie Huilin was the first to kick. Her ball made it past goalkeeper Briana Scurry. Next, Team USA's Carla Overbeck faked out keeper Gao Hong. Overbeck drove the ball to Hong's left, but Hong went to the right and the ball went into the net. Qui Haiyan and Joy Fawcett each made their goals. At this point, the score was 2–2.

Next up from China was Liu Ying. Ying kicked the ball and Scurry dove and knocked the ball away from the net. The spectators exploded! Scurry made the one save that Team USA

Xie Huilin

needed. Then Kristine Lilly made her shot— United States 3–China 2. Zhang Ouying of China got her shot past Scurry. The score: 3–3. Mia Hamm, one of the most beloved players on the '99ers team, strode forward. With great determination, she blasted the ball into the net.

United States 4–China 3.

Kristine Lilly

Each team had one kicker left. Could the pressure get any higher? China had to score, or the United States would win the World Cup. Sun Yen was the last kicker for China. She sent the ball flying into the net! China 4–United States 4. Winning this World Cup now rested on the shoulders of the last US player—Brandi Chastain.

To confuse China's keeper, US coach Tony DiCicco told Chastain to kick the ball with her left foot even though she had never done that before in a match. He had seen her at practices kicking the ball with her weaker foot. He believed she could do it, but he was taking a big risk. Chastain placed the ball and coolly kicked with her left foot. The ball soared past Hong and landed just inside the left goalpost.

The onlookers could not contain themselves. Chastain pulled off her shirt, fell to her knees in her sports bra, and screamed joyously! The United States had just won the 1999 World Cup on home soil. They were Women's World Cup champions for the second time. The '99ers became immediate heroes for generations to come. Brandi Chastain's iconic photo was seen on the covers of *Newsweek* and *Sports Illustrated* as well as in many other magazines and newspapers around the world!

Endorsement Deals

For the fifteen months before the 1999 Women's World Cup took place, Brandi Chastain had been under contract with Nike. When asked, she told Nike clothing designers exactly what she wanted in a sports bra. When she ripped off her shirt after her World Cup-winning kick, she was wearing the sports bra she helped design. Nike rushed the new bra into production.

This led to other endorsement deals. She was featured on the Wheaties box, and she appeared in television commercials for Nike, Bud Light, and Gatorade.

Chastain earned about $2 million from her endorsements. That's a lot of money. But top male athletes at the time were signing $90 million endorsement deals!

CHAPTER 6
Changing of the Guard

In 2003, the Women's World Cup had to be moved from China, the original host country, to the United States. It was because of the epidemic of the SARS (severe acute respiratory syndrome) virus that had hit China. Since the United States had hosted the tournament in 1999, they were prepared to host again.

This World Cup signaled a changing of the guard. It marked the start of the incredible careers of American Abby Wambach and Brazil's Marta Vieira da Silva, known as Marta the GOAT (Greatest of All Time). Team USA showcased the next generation of stars, like Aly Wagner, Cat Reddick, and Shannon Boxx. And to see Abby Wambach and Mia Hamm play

Abby Wambach

together on the same field was nothing short of amazing!

It was the last World Cup tournament for Mia Hamm, Brandi Chastain, Julie Foudy, and

Julie Foudy

Joy Fawcett. In the group games, Abby Wambach immediately emerged as a star, scoring two goals, one against Nigeria and the other against North Korea.

This Women's World Cup was also the beginning of an outstanding period for the German team. In the quarterfinals, Germany smashed Russia, 7–1. In the game between the United States and Norway, Wambach scored the game's only goal on a header. Cat Reddick took a free kick and lobbed it in front of the goal where Wambach headed the ball. It bounced off the hand of the Norwegian goalkeeper and went into the lower right corner of the net. The United States knocked Norway out of the World Cup!

German team

In the semifinal, Germany beat Team USA, 3–0. The United States was stunned to lose on home soil. But the team finished the tournament in third place.

During the final game, Sweden led 1–0 at halftime against Germany. But that score didn't last long. Germany's Maren Meinert tied the game just one minute into the second half. The score stayed at 1–1 through the ninetieth minute and the game went into extra time. At minute ninety-eight, Nia Künzer headed in the winning goal—a Golden Goal. Germany

Tina Theune-Meyer

won, and Tina Theune-Meyer became the first female coach to win the World Cup!

The End of an Era

Mia Hamm was the first international star of women's soccer. She played on the US Women's National Team that competed in four FIFA Women's World Cups—1991, 1995, 1999, and 2003, winning in 1991 and 1999.

Hamm retired from the national team with 158 goals in international competition, the most by any player, male or female, at that time. FIFA named Hamm Women's World Player of the Year in 2001 and 2002. Jerseys with her number 9 became a top seller.

After she retired, she founded the Mia Hamm Foundation to raise money for cord blood transplants and women's youth soccer. She is also a co-owner of the Los Angeles Football Club (LAFC).

CHAPTER 7
Controversy!

In 2007, China hosted the women's World Cup tournament for the second time. In the group stage, Germany trounced Argentina, 11–0. This was the first double-digit score at a World Cup. It was also the largest score difference in the history of the World Cup up to this point. Team USA played against Brazil in the semifinals. Having never won a World Cup, Brazil desperately wanted to win this game. And, of course, the United States had also set their sights on winning.

Legendary goalkeeper Hope Solo made her debut in this World Cup tournament at the age of twenty-six. She had replaced veteran keeper Briana Scurry, who remained on the team.

Solo started in every match of the group games as well as the first match against England in the quarterfinals.

Head coach Greg Ryan thought he knew how Team USA could beat Brazil. He decided to take Solo out

Hope Solo

in the semifinals and play Scurry as goalkeeper. Ryan made this decision because Scurry had played Brazil's national team twelve times and had won each game, including the 2004 Olympics gold-medal match. He believed that Scurry understood how Brazil played and would be better than Solo at anticipating the Brazilian players' moves. However, what Ryan didn't account for was that Scurry had never faced 21-year-old Marta! With Scurry in the goal, the United States lost 4–0. This was their worst loss in the Women's

Marta

National Team history. It ended their fifty-one-game winning streak.

Solo was fuming. When reporters interviewed her, she said, "It was the wrong decision, and I think anybody who knows anything about the game knows that. There's no doubt in my mind I would have made those saves. And the fact of the matter is, it's not 2004 anymore."

Her teammates were shocked at what Solo said. That night back at the hotel, members of the team confronted her. Solo said the comment was directed at Greg Ryan, not at Briana Scurry.

She immediately apologized to Scurry, but Scurry didn't forgive Solo. The players hashed out their feelings and agreed that Solo must apologize to the entire team. Solo did, but no one believed she was sincere. The decision was made to suspend her. Solo would not be allowed to play in the third-place match game. Also, she couldn't even go to the game. She couldn't eat her meals with the team or fly home on the same plane. Solo's suspension lasted a year. She returned to the team as starting goalkeeper in the 2008 Olympics. However, Solo still found herself resented by some of her team members.

In the match for third place in 2007, Team USA played against Norway. "This match is our chance to get back on the field and show our country and our fans how we can play soccer," said team captain Kristine Lilly, veteran of five World Cups and one of the most accomplished athletes in women's soccer history, having played in all fifty matches with Team USA from the 1988 International Women's Football Tournament through three Olympics to 2007's match for third place in the Women's World Cup. She was trying to help her team put their loss to Brazil behind them. It worked! The United States beat Norway, 4–1.

United States vs. Norway, 2007

While the US women did win third place, the World Cup went to Germany.

Germany became the first team to win back-to-back Women's World Cups!

Throughout the entire tournament, not a single goal was scored against Germany because of the phenomenal German goalkeeper Nadine Angerer! She played all 540 minutes of the tournament. No one in the history of the World Cup, men's or women's, had ever matched this achievement. In the final, she saved a penalty kick from Marta, who had scored seven goals in the tournament. Angerer won the Golden Glove award for best goalkeeper. Marta won the Golden Boot and the Golden Ball and led Brazil to a second-place finish.

Nadine Angerer

Kristine Lilly

This was the first Women's World Cup in which all teams received bonuses according to the last round they reached. The champions were to split $1 million, runners-up $800,000, third place $650,000, fourth place $550,000, quarterfinalists $300,000, and first-round exits $200,000. As a comparison, the lowest bonuses for men's teams in the 2006 World Cup were more than $7 million, with the champions receiving nearly $30 million! The women's teams still had a great deal of work ahead of them to be paid equally. It took until 2022 to see that happen.

Team USA wins the 2019 Women's World Cup.

Fans in Washington, DC, watch the 2019 Women's World Cup final.

Team USA wins the 1991 Women's World Cup.

Norway (red) plays against Germany (white) in the 1995 final.

Mia Hamm (#9) of USA plays in the 1999 final against China.

Brandi Chastain celebrates kicking the winning goal at the
1999 Women's World Cup finals.

Michelle Akers wins FIFA's Female Player of the Century award in 2000.

The Women's World Cup trophy

China (white) and Norway (red) play in the 2007 Women's World Cup.

Satoshi Takahashi/LightRocket/Getty Images

The wreckage of the 2011 earthquake and tsunami in Japan

Japan celebrates winning the 2011 Women's World Cup by thanking their fans.

Team USA waves to the crowd at the 2015 Women's World Cup semifinal game.

Carli Lloyd is awarded the Golden Ball trophy in 2015.

Marta during the 2019 Women's World Cup

Nettie Honeyball

Players of the Dick, Kerr's Ladies team warm up before a game.

Lily Parr hits the ball with her head.

Mexico's women's national football team before the unofficial
1971 Women's World Cup in Mexico City

CHAPTER 8
GOAT

Marta is considered the GOAT (Greatest of All Time) of women's football. She grew up very poor in Dois Riachos, Brazil. She started out playing football barefoot with her brothers. She sharpened her skills as a young girl by kicking around balls she made from rolled-up grocery bags.

She played on boys' soccer teams, wearing oversized cleats stuffed with paper in the toes because there weren't any girls' sizes in Dois Riachos. Marta played in boys' school leagues until the day a coach refused to let his team compete in a regional tournament unless she withdrew.

What did Marta do?

She walked away from the game so that her team could continue to play.

Marta eventually joined a local boys' junior

 team. That was when a scout discovered her. He was looking to start a women's team. So, at age fourteen, having never left home, she boarded a bus to Rio de Janeiro.

The city was on the other side of her country. She would play for this new team. But within a few years, the club closed.

Since there weren't enough opportunities for her in Brazil, she moved overseas to Sweden. Women's football was taken seriously there. She played for four years in Sweden and then moved to the United States. On occasion, she returned to Brazil to play for super-footballer Pelé's Santos women's team.

Marta made her international debut in 2003 as a member of Brazil's under-twenty Women's World Cup team (a team for players under the age of twenty). To this day, she continues to play for Brazil in World Cup tournaments. Marta has incredible skills, dazzling both players and fans. Her desire to win means she never gives up a chance to score a goal. She has received FIFA's World Player of the Year award six times. In 2019, she became the first player—male or female—to score in five World Cups. She also holds the title of leading World Cup scorer of all time. Despite never taking home a World Cup medal for Brazil, Marta has influenced an entire generation of young female soccer players.

Not only is Marta a fighter on the pitch, but she also pushes players and fans to be more inclusive (to include everyone, allowing people who in the past have been excluded because of their race, gender, sexuality, or ability). Along with many of her teammates around the world, she has been extremely vocal about equal pay and equal opportunity.

CHAPTER 9
An Emotional World Cup

In 2011, the Japanese Women's World Cup team had to make an extremely difficult decision.

On March 11 of that year, a 9.0 magnitude earthquake hit the northeast coast of Japan. Within thirty minutes, a powerful tsunami (a huge tidal wave usually caused by an earthquake under the sea) struck the coast with massive thirty-foot waves. Almost twenty thousand people lost

their lives or went missing. Thousands of buildings were destroyed. Hundreds of thousands of people were forced from their homes. Three reactors at a nuclear power plant melted down. This caused radiation to leak into the area. (People get sick and can die from exposure to radiation.) It was one of Japan's worst natural disasters.

Now the Japanese women's football team had to decide what to do. Should they go to Germany and compete in the 2011 World Cup?

Yes! The players and coaches agreed to go to Germany. They wanted to raise the spirits and give hope to the people of their country.

In Germany, Japan had a strong start in the group stage. The team came in a close second behind England. Japan had never made it out of the group stage before.

In the quarterfinal, Japan faced Germany, the host country. Germany was the stronger team and favored to win.

Right before the quarterfinal match, Coach Norio Sasaki showed slides of the destruction back home. The photographs were vivid reminders of why the team was competing. Japan was determined to win.

Karina Maruyama

After a tense ninety minutes of play, the score was 0–0. By the end of the first half of extra time, the score was still 0–0. Then, three minutes into the second half, Karina Maruyama scored the winning, and only, goal. She was one of two Japanese players who had worked at the nuclear power plant before the meltdown. Japan beat Germany, 1–0!

In the semifinal, Japan beat Sweden, 3–1. Japan had made it through to the final!

Who would Japan be competing against in the final? The powerful, two-time (1991 and 1999) World Cup–winning US team! After twelve years,

the United States was playing in a final game once
more. The stronger, taller US team took control
right from the beginning. They kept the ball on
Japan's side of the field and many players—Carli
Lloyd, Megan Rapinoe, Abby Wambach, and
Lauren Cheney—pounded shots to the goal from
different angles on the pitch. At minute sixty-
nine, Alex Morgan shot the ball into the net!
United States 1–Japan 0.

But Japan would not give up. Japan tied
the game, forcing the match into extra time.

Wambach scored, but as the match clock wound down, Japanese team captain Homare Sawa hit a shot that bounced off Wambach and past the keeper, Hope Solo, into the net. The score after extra time was United States 2–Japan 2. The championship rested on a penalty shoot-out!

The United States missed their first three penalty shots. Then Wambach made her shot. Japan got three goals past Hope Solo. Final goal count: Japan 3–United States 1. The Japanese team won the 2011 World Cup, and they were ecstatic!

They were the first country from Asia to win the trophy. They had played their hearts out for the people of Japan.

"We played that tournament not only for ourselves," said Ayumi Kaihori, Japan's goalkeeper. "We felt we had not only the support of Japan, but also the whole world."

After winning, the players showed their immense appreciation by carrying a banner around the field that read: *To Our Friends Around the World, Thank You for Your Support.*

What a team! What a tournament!

CHAPTER 10
Breaking Records

In 2019, the USWNT had an incredible series in France. Throughout the month, they dominated their opponents. In the tournament opener, Alex Morgan, the team's star striker, scored five goals as the United States swept Thailand with a 13–0 win! Morgan, being the team player that she is, also made three assists, the most for one player in a single Women's World Cup game.

Alex Morgan

In the second group game, the United States played against Chile. Carli Lloyd scored at minute eleven and became the first player to score in six straight Women's World Cup matches. Then in minute thirty-five, she scored again— her tenth World Cup goal! The United States beat Chile, 3–0.

In the last group game, Team USA played Sweden. At minute three, Megan Rapinoe sent a low bouncing corner kick to Lindsey Horan, who got it into the net for the first goal of the game. In the second half, an own goal was made by Sweden's Jonna Andersson and the United States beat Sweden, 2–0. (An own goal occurs when a soccer player kicks a ball into her own net or goal and the opposing team is awarded a point.)

On the hottest day ever recorded in France (114° F), more than forty-five thousand screaming fans cheered on two of the World Cup's favorite teams during the quarterfinals. The United States competed against France. Rapinoe scored twice. With a 2–1 win, Team USA reached the semifinals for the eighth straight time!

Megan Rapinoe

In the eighty-fourth minute of the hair-raising semifinal game against England, goalkeeper Alyssa Naeher dove to her right and saved a penalty kick off the foot of England's Steph Houghton without allowing a rebound. Naeher saved Team USA's 2–1 lead. Next up, the final!

Nearly 57,900 spectators gathered in France's Grand Stade de Lyon to watch Team USA's championship match against the Netherlands. By the end of the first half, the score was 0–0. In the second half, Rapinoe made the first goal at minute sixty-one from the penalty spot. Newcomer and breakout star Rose Lavelle then brought the United States to its 2–0 victory at minute sixty-nine. With this win, the USWNT earned its second straight World Cup victory and its fourth World Cup win—the most wins in Women's World Cup history! Rapinoe received the Golden Boot for scoring the most goals and the Golden Ball for being the best overall player in the finals.

The good news is that

today women's soccer is a global phenomenon!

What caused this?

The way the United States Women's National Team plays the game! Besides four World Cups, they have won four Olympic gold medals. More important, they fill stadiums with their energy and without the unpleasantness that can happen during men's games. Although there are fouls (for careless play), yellow cards (for reckless play), and red cards (for reckless force and an automatic ejection) in women's soccer, they are not given out as frequently as in men's games. Women have fewer injuries. Male players often fake injuries and stall for time. In women's games, there is no fighting and pushing around.

The 2015 FIFA Women's World Cup Final in Canada was the most-watched soccer game in United States history, and more than 1.12 billion people worldwide watched the 2019 FIFA Women's World Cup played in France.

It's strange that the United States and not England—where the game was invented—is leading the way in the world of women's soccer. Much of its popularity can be attributed to the 1999 team. That's when women's soccer became big global news. When the '99ers were invited to the White House, President Bill Clinton said that women's soccer "is going to have a bigger impact than people ever realize, and it will have a far-reaching impact not only in the United States but also in other countries."

He was right. Today, there are an estimated 30 million women playing soccer worldwide. Female sports announcers are commentating on men's and women's soccer games and female officials are now presiding over some of the world's top male tournaments.

CHAPTER 11
Equal Pay

After the United States won the 2019 Women's World Cup, the sold-out crowd burst into cheers. Then the fans shouted, "Equal Pay! Equal Pay!" when the FIFA president presented the medals to the players. The same thing happened in New York City, where there was a ticker-tape parade for the team. US women's players once again set their sights on fighting for equal pay.

The pay breakdown of the World Cup prize money between the 2018 Men's World Cup and the 2019 Women's World Cup was:

World Cup Year	Total Prize Money / Winner's Prize
2018 (men)	$400 million for 32 teams / $38 million
2019 (women)	$30 million for 24 teams / $4 million

Cocaptain Megan Rapinoe said, "We put on the most incredible show that you could ever ask for. We can't do anything more to impress more, to be better ambassadors, to take on more, to play better . . . It's time to move that conversation forward to the next step." Along with other women soccer players including cocaptain Alex Morgan, Rapinoe has always been outspoken and has fought hard for fairness in the sport.

There has been a long history of friction between the USWNT and the USSF (the United States Soccer Federation) that dates to 1996. The USWNT players threatened to boycott (refuse to attend) the Olympics over wages. In March 2019, twenty-eight members of the USWNT filed a lawsuit against the USSF. The group claimed they were being treated differently based on their gender. For women soccer players, not only were their paychecks affected, but also where they competed and how often, what kind of surface they played on, how they trained, the medical treatment and coaching they received, and even the kind of hotels they stayed at.

In 2020, the USSF and the USWNT resolved the players' claims about working conditions. Now the question of equal pay needed to be resolved.

In 2022, a decision was finally made. The women soccer players were awarded $22 million in back pay. In addition, $2 million was placed

in a fund for businesses and charities with which retired women players become involved. Along with this, the USWNT would be given the same rate of pay and bonuses as the men's teams going forward for all games including the World Cup! This was a long-overdue victory for women soccer players in the United States.

Upon hearing the news, Megan Rapinoe said, "For us as players, I'm just so proud of the way we stuck together. . . . For us this is just a huge win in ensuring that we not only right the wrongs of the past but set the next generation up for something that we could only have dreamed of."

CHAPTER 12
Soccer Is for All

Female soccer players have had to fight hard for more than equal pay. In 2007, Asmahan Mansour, a footballer from Ontario, wanted to wear a hijab while playing in a tournament. A hijab is a head covering worn by some Muslim girls and women. The referee told her that she  could remove the hijab and play, but it would not be permitted on the pitch. Her team withdrew from the match to show their support for her.

The issue went to FIFA. It was decided that wearing a hijab was dangerous even though there was no data that proved wearing one could strangle a player or injure an opponent. The result was that Mansour did not play. Nor did thousands of girls and women for almost seven years afterward!

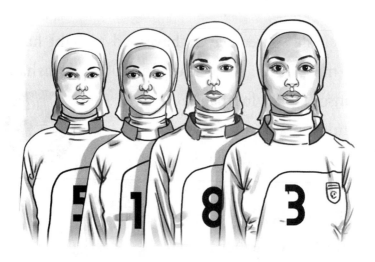

This same issue came up in 2011 in an Olympic qualifying match—Iran against Jordan. The Iranian team was wearing hijabs that they believed met FIFA's new rules for shorter hijabs, but FIFA didn't agree, so the women were banned from playing. Heartbroken and frustrated, the team from Iran left the pitch.

Players and fans—male and female—from around the world put pressure on FIFA. Sportswear companies designed hijabs that resolved all the supposed safety questions.

Finally, on March 1, 2014, FIFA announced that religious head coverings would be allowed. It was an important moment.

The story of women's soccer and the World Cup continues. Each generation has paved the way for the next. With more countries involved in the game and up-and-coming players starting each year, soccer is sure to give us more hat tricks, headers, penalty kicks, and heart-stopping plays.

Timeline of the Women's World Cup

1895 — The first women's football (soccer) match by FA rules is played; North London beats South London, 7–1

1921 — The FA bans women from playing in England on the grounds that it's unhealthy

1971 — The FA Council lifts the ban on women's matches

1991 — First FIFA World Championship for Women's Football is played in China; Team USA beats Norway, 2–1

1995 — Second Women's World Cup is played in Sweden; Norway beats Germany, 2–0

1999 — Third Women's World Cup is held in the United States; Team USA beats China, 5–4

2003 — Fourth Women's World Cup is again played in the United States; Germany beats Sweden, 2–1

2007 — Fifth Women's World Cup is played in China; Germany wins second World Cup title in a row

2011 — Sixth Women's World Cup is played in Germany

2015 — Seventh Women's World Cup is played in Canada; Team USA beats Japan, 5–2

2019 — Eighth Women's World Cup is played in France; Team USA beats the Netherlands, 2–0 for their fourth World Cup win

Timeline of the World

1895	Legendary baseball player George Herman Ruth Jr., nicknamed Babe Ruth, born in Baltimore, Maryland
1920	The Nineteenth Amendment giving women the right to vote is ratified in the United States
1971	Walt Disney World opens in Orlando, Florida
1986	The fourth reactor at the Chernobyl nuclear power plant explodes, causing the world's worst nuclear disaster to date
1988	The first female prime minister of the United Kingdom, Margaret Thatcher, becomes the longest-serving Prime Minister of the twentieth century
1995	Frenchwoman Jeanne Calment becomes the oldest person in history as she turns 120 years and 238 days old on October 17. Calment will live to be 122 years and 164 days old
1999	The number of internet users worldwide reaches 150 million; more than 50 percent are in the United States
2007	Nancy Pelosi is elected first female speaker of the House as Democrats take control of Congress
2019	China's robotic space probe Chang'e 4 becomes the first spacecraft in history to land in the South Pole–Aitken Basin region, known as the "far side" or "dark side" of the moon

Bibliography

*Books for young readers

*Christopher, Matt. ***World Cup: An Action-Packed Look at Soccer's Biggest Competition***. New York: Little, Brown and Company, 2018.

*Christopher, Matt. ***On the Field with . . . Megan Rapinoe, Alex Morgan, Carli Lloyd, Mallory Pugh***. New York: Little, Brown and Company, 2020.

*Clarke, Catriona. ***She Shoots, She Scores! A Celebration of Women's Soccer***. New York: Kingfisher, 2021.

Debakcsy, Dale. "An All Too Brief History of the Women's World Cup." ***Women You Should Know***. June 27, 2019. https://womenyoushouldknow.net/history-womens-world-cup/.

ESPNsoccernet. "History of the FIFA Women's World Cup." September 6, 2007. https://www.active.com/soccer/articles/history-of-the-fifa-women-s-world-cup.

FIFA World Football Museum. ***The Official History of the FIFA Women's World Cup: The Story of Women's Football From 1881 to the Present***. London: Carlton Books, 2019.

Hardy, James. "Goal: The Story of How Women's Soccer Rose to Fame." ***History Cooperative***. September 15, 2016. https://historycooperative.org/goal-the-story-of-how-womens-soccer-rose-to-fame/.

Lloyd, Carli, with Wayne Coffey. ***When Nobody Was Watching: My Hard-Fought Journey to the Top of the Soccer World***. New York: Houghton Mifflin Harcourt, 2016.

Murray, Caitlin. ***The National Team: The Inside Story of the Women Who Changed Soccer***. New York: Abrams Press, 2019.

National Football Museum. "The Fascinating History of the Women's World Cup." Google Arts & Culture. https://artsandculture.google.com/exhibit/the-fascinating-history-of-the-women-s-world-cup-nationalfootballmuseum/KALiGYa-UKS_Lw?hl=en.

Rapinoe, Megan, with Emma Brockes. ***One Life***. New York: Penguin Press, 2021.

Soccer Politics. "History of the Women's World Cup: Tournament Guides." Duke University, 2015, https://sites.duke.edu/wcwp/tournament-guides/world-cup-2015-guide/history-of-the-womens-world-cup/.

Solo, Hope, with Ann Killion. ***Solo: A Memoir of Hope***. New York: HarperCollins Publishers, 2012.

Street Football World. "A Woman's Game: The First-Ever Women's World Cup." February 19, 2018. https://www.streetfootballworld.org/latest/blog/woman-s-game-first-ever-women-s-world-cup.

Theivam, Kieran, and Jeff Kassouf. *The Making of the Women's World Cup: Defining Stories from a Sport's Coming of Age*. London: Robinson, 2019.

Turner, Morgan. "Past Women's World Cup Champions." *Sports Illustrated*. June 7, 2019. https://www.si.com/soccer/2019/06/07/womens-world-cup-winners-list-past-champions-finals.

*Walters, Meg. *World Cup Women: Megan, Alex, and the Team USA Soccer Champs*. Illustrated by Nikkolas Smith. New York: Sky Pony Press, 2019.

*Wambach, Abby. *Forward: My Story, Young Readers' Edition*. New York: HarperCollins Publishers, 2016.